MW01254426

The Hardship Post

Poems by Jehanne Dubrow

three candles press

2009

threecandlespress.com

The Hardship Post

Contents

NOTES

Library of Congress Control Number: 2008911575
Author's Photo: Jeremy Schaub
Book Design: Steve Mueske

Acknowledgements

American Poetry Journal: "Baggage"
Artful Dodge: "Yahrzeit"
Barrow Street: "In Vicenza"
Blackbird: "Charm Against a Broken Tongue" in an earlier version
Burnside Review: "Bone-Blind"
Carolina Quarterly: "Rosh Hashanah"
Cincinnati Review: "With the Interpreter"
Diner: "Baba Jaga"
Eleventh Muse: "Rehmuh Synagogue, Poland"
Florida Review: "Going South"
Folio: "At the Holocaust Conference"
Gulf Coast: "Third Generation"
Hudson Review: "Cinderella" and "Rave"
Innisfree Poetry Journal: "Basia"
Judaism: "Judaic Studies"
Kerem: "Sukkot"
Margie: "Mistaken for a Gypsy Girl"
Measure: "Tashlikh"
Mezzo Cammin: "Always Already," "The Amber Brooch," "A Brief Ontology
        of Guilt," "Diplomat's Daughter," "Old Town," and "Voyeurs"
Midstream: "The Stone I Found At Auschwitz"
New England Review: "Fasting"
New Works Review: "The Language Thief" and "Lot's Wife in Eastern Europe"
Poetry: "The Izaak Synagogue" and "Souvenir"
Poetry Northwest: "Discussing Miłosz"
Shenandoah: "Bargaining with the Wolf"
Southeast Review: "All Saints' Day"
Tikkun: "Mezuzah"
Three Candles Journal: "At Mel Krupin's," "Icon of the Black Madonna,"
        and "Kosher Dills"
Umbrella: "Zeno's Paradox of the Shtetl"

"Bone-Blind" was awarded an honorable mention in the *Atlantic Monthly* Student Writers' Competition.

"Discussing Miłosz," was awarded 2nd-place in the *Atlantic Monthly* Student Writers' Competition.

"Mistaken for a Gypsy Girl" was selected as a finalist in the *Margie* Strong Rx Medicine Poetry Contest.

"My Mother, Making Piroshke" was awarded a Dorothy Sargent Rosenberg award. Published on the Dorothy Sargent Rosenberg Memorial fund website under the title "Making Piroshke."

"Ossuary" was awarded an honorable mention in the Anna Davidson Rosenberg Awards for Poems on the Jewish Experience, published on the San Francisco Jewish Community Center website.

"Souvenir" appears in the essay "On Remembering 'Souvenir,'" which is part of the anthology, *Poem, Revised* (Vocabula Books).

"Tashlikh" was included in the exhibit "Art from the Ashes," held at the Osher Marin Jewish Community Center, in San Rafael, California. An alternate version of the poem appeared in the exhibit, "The Lost Shabbos: The Jews of Oświęcim," which was created for the Auschwitz Jewish Center, in Oświęcim, Poland.

*

This book was made possible by funds granted to the author through a Sosland Foundation Fellowship at the Center for Advanced Holocaust Studies, United States Holocaust Memorial Museum. The statements made and views expressed, however, are solely the responsibility of the author.

I am extremely grateful for the support of the Center for Advanced Holocaust Studies, the Harris Center for Judaic Studies, the Summer Institute on the Holocaust and Jewish Civilization, the Nebraska Summer Writer's Conference, and the University of Nebraska-Lincoln.

I also want to thank the poets, teachers, and friends who have so encouraged me and who have helped to shape this book: Grace Bauer, Kelly Grey Carlisle, Michael Collier, Helene Fischman, Charles Fishman, Leslie Harrison, Sheila Jelen, Ted Kooser, Kristin Naca, Ruth Nisse, Alicia Suskin Ostriker, Stanley Plumly, Hilda Raz, Gerald Shapiro, Vincent Slatt, Yerra Sugarman, Alan Steinweis, and Joshua Weiner. And thank you to Steve Mueske of Three Candles Press—without your support of my work, there would be no collection.

Finally, my love and thanks to my parents, Jeannette and Stephen Dubrow, to my brother Eric, and to my puppy Argos. And to my husband Jeremy, I love you in the whole wide world.

1

EXILE'S FAIRY TALE

Her bed stretches its legs each night,
    spreads ornamental claws to creep
across a carpet thick as grass.
      The queen-sized mattress barely shakes
its passenger. She's fast asleep,
        her eyelids brushed with powdered glass.
Which skyline does she dream then wake
    beneath? Which sorcery? The lights
of a foreign city, the ache,
    lodged like a shuttle-point deep
beneath her skin—these are the birthrights
      of refugees. She trespasses
but never finds a place to rest,
      each night the uninvited guest.

CINDERELLA

Mistranslated, fur slippers became glass,
the *vair* transforming into *verre*, with no
concern for how the change might change the girl.

And so she tiptoed to the ball, limping
because her feet weren't used to crystal heels.
She danced despite the blisters on her toes

and blood, a stain inside transparent shoes.
The waltz couldn't end soon enough. Then guests
surrounded her to admire how she turned

a phrase, how language filtered through her mouth
in careful streams. She said, "How do you do?"
almost as if the words were hers at birth.

The words had taken months to learn (*bateau*
became a boat, *chapeau* a hat) and months
before the accent shifted on her tongue

and settled into place. Sipping champagne,
she missed her other fairytale, when warm
fur coverings had cushioned every tread—

the fur, less glamorous than glass but more
secure than this translated, English life
that ends with shards left on the palace steps.

THE DIPLOMAT'S DAUGHTER

She drinks the tea, her lips kissing the bone
edge of the china cup, a sip so fine
and smooth, rehearsed as choreography.
Her pinky angles just the right degree.
Who taught her to sit like a princess,
glass-still while conversations spin across
the room? Small drops that trickle from her mouth,
falling onto the linen tablecloth,
glint like citrines before they disappear.
She could almost be the girl in a Vermeer:
posed, a face of painted porcelain
that catches light, her glowing underskin.
Except, while no one looks, incisors snap
against her tongue, the closing of a trap.

IN VICENZA

Thirty years ago, my mother ate a poisoned slice
of gorgonzola, and I was born, knifing

from that womb, a luminescent world,
where I once curled

my body like a fern. It's just another place I don't recall
for all its resonance, awful

and darkly beautiful, a landmark learned then lost,
as though the cost

of too much journeying must be amnesia.
Returning to Palladio's loggias,

I follow corridors that fuse with rooms
subsumed by other rooms.

The marble echoes underneath my feet.
I hear the heartbeat

of a ticking clock. A wall's
pierced openings let sunlight fall

across the floor in slivered marks,
so that I cross from day to dark

and back again, always the visitor
through passageways both bright and sinister.

BARGAINING WITH THE WOLF

Sometimes, I hear you growl behind
the doors of sleep. And never mind
that it's been twenty years (or more
than that) since meadows greened my floor
and Grandfather dragged Peter home,
where no trombone or kettledrum
could reach the boy. I heard
the flute which fluttered like a bird,
the clarinet on feline paws,
the oboe-duck. And then, because
I was afraid to stop the tape
(too slow to pause) a silver shape
crept out, its canines glistening
with blood. I sat there listening,
my fingers pressing shut my ears.
I even hear you now. Old fears
still nibble with the sharpest teeth,
your three French horns, a leitmotif
that circles in the night and waits
for me to dream. When I was eight
(or nine) I buried the cassette
in the corner of my closet,
beneath a heap of outgrown clothes,
as if my phobia (enclosed,
secluded in a cubbyhole)
could shrink down to the size of a mole,
a velvet form which finds its way
by scenting through the black. Some days,
your growl is closer to a groan
(it must be hard to live alone,

that closet tighter than it was
before, no space to hone your claws).
Perhaps you hate sealed places just
as much as I. If I could trust
you not to frighten me or bite,
I would unchain the door. The nights
are orchestras. Stringed voices speak
domestic mysteries. Mice squeak.
The moon shines moderato on
my bedroom walls until the dawn.
The world's been tamed—your fangs are white
as though you seldom kill, twilight
now hums a stranger violence.
I hate these bloodless cadences.
Teach me to howl, to bay, to bark
new terrors prowling through the dark.

BONE-BLIND

Zaire, 1977

She can't remember. So they have told her
rainstorms turned the Congo River black.
They've told her the houseboy smeared the gates
with red, casting a spell in chicken's blood

to keep bad men away. That she couldn't sleep.
Her crib glowed green, the walls and ceiling lit
by neon spiders, large as dinner plates.
That the moon kept her awake with night terrors.

It hung like a white fist over the house,
ready to smash the roof. *Regarde, la lune.*
That pine trees bent like mourners in the wind.
Or, in the dry season, the woods stood stiff

as if marking rows and rows of graves.
And that she didn't learn to walk outdoors.
Black mambas nested by the pool, coiled
nooses at the shallow end, the ropes that bite.

They've told her that the term is hardship post
when there's extra pay and risk of war.
That they elbowed through the crowds of beggars
who clogged the entrance to the consulate.

That they bought a bag of jewelry from one:
baubles carved from the tusks of elephants,
the ivory cut and the bodies left to rot.
That they gave the smallest bracelet to her

though she can't remember ever wearing it.
But she must have—what a lucky little girl
to slip the present on her wrist, the bone,
leaving its bleached shadow on her skin.

VOYEURS
Brussels, 1994

Near the careful lines of the Grand Place, the pink
and purple canopies, the marble child

forever pissing in his marble sink,
we ate the perfect Belgian meal of *frites*

with mayonnaise and *moules* cooked in white wine
and endive served with mustard vinaigrette.

My mother talked about cables dispatched
from Africa. Two groups, she said between bites,

the Hutus and Tutsis. At first we laughed,
the names like made-up words in schoolyard songs,

or sounds a baby makes, vowels liquefied
like chocolate truffles melting on the tongue.

Machetes, she explained, to hack hundreds
in half as quickly as a knife slices

a plate of greens. Or else the crooked blade
that short tribes use to cut the cockroaches

(the taller tribes) and bring them down to size.
Some worshippers were kneeling in a church.

First, doors were barred, torches lit outside,
then fire swallowed air. We closed our eyes.

Man's inhumanity to man, we sighed,
ate crème brûlée to sate our appetite.

BABA JAGA
the witch of Slavic folklore

I felt along the fence of human bone,
the keyhole with its maw of teeth, the key
that bit right back if turned too suddenly
inside the lock. She walked me through her home,

showed me how to nip my words in two,
like doubled cherries split apart, spilling
each vowel into a bowl, a hollowed skull
that held wet pits. And what about the juice?

Her spittle wrote red letters on the floor.
You'll learn to speak, she said, *as I have taught
myself.* She hexed the stars to stutter out,
our only light now traces of her tours

across the sky, then kicked away a broom
so that it brushed the edges of my sleep,
the branches of the silver birch, a snap
of twigs, which echoed in my waking room.

RAVE

For one night I'm disguised as one of them,
        dressed to blend in with other dancing limbs,

the arms and legs that slide and shift inside
        the sound like paper chains tangled by wind.

A woman tells me how the music splits
        her brain apart from everything, the hips

whose heaviness she hates, the dangling weight
        of her breasts. She's waited for this metal beat

that frees her to do anything: to fuck
        in some dark room or swallow pills or sink,

her thoughts like nitrous balloons floating away.
        Words are limiting, she says. And who am I

to say, *You're wrong. Words are all we've got.*
        I don't belong where bodies separate

from minds like sand trying to leave behind
        the sea—I should shout, *The body is too cold*

a place to stay inside, unless we speak.
        I dance. Tomorrow, light will make me sick.

I'll wash the glitter from my face, pick
        sleep out of my eyes, and walk to work.

MISTAKEN FOR A GYPSY GIRL

Poland, 1981

My braids were two black ropes,
my coat red-berry red.
Ahead, a boy looked back,
his cheeks like sharpened points
that almost broke the skin.

His mother caught me staring.
She made the cross, each hand
a razor through the air.
Easy to guess her thoughts—
all gypsy girls are thieves

—I'd stood in many lines,
each one the same, the soot
that stained the sky to gray,
the dull smell of December.
I'd stood in many lines,

my hair a raven's wing,
my eyes not Polish lakes
of blue. *Romany,* they said,
letting me cut the line
to buy a seedless rye,

and a pastry fat with jam.
Their hands reached past to grope
the rosary of my braids.
They whispered *run away.*
I was the child in the woods

who knows that even day
is dangerous, the world
a briar patch of thorns
and poisoned fruit, ovens
that open into fire,

and orphans baked like cakes.
But the bread still tasted safe,
like a road leading home.
Beneath my shirt, a Jewish star
burned yellow in my skin.

THE LANGUAGE THIEF

Some hands she left as stumps. Some hands she left
but took the tongues instead, her cut so deft

our throats still opened for another sigh.
She pried

the first pearl tooth
from baby's mouth.

Before, we kept our homes unlocked, although
good prophecies had fled a year ago.

Next year, Jerusalem, we wept
into our cups. We slept

that night while she chewed
bitter herbs, gargled our few

leftover tears. We slept while she wiped blood
from lintel-frames, the fluid thick as mud.

She opened wide
the doors   and let the Angel step inside.

2

ZENO'S PARADOX OF THE SHTETL

It is the frozen world that I've approached
for thirty years but cannot reach—

halfway
to Poland in a sleigh,

imagining the silver runners crossing
permafrost,

and halfway to Galicia again,
passing the wooden synagogues, men

who wear black coats and fur-trimmed hats,
their wives and daughters fat

with goosedown layers,
mittens, scarves, babushkas covering black hair,

the women's faces lined, opaque,
a pewter sheet of ice above a lake,

and halfway to a town that shivers by
the Vistula, the river's luminosity

like fish scales scraped
away with knives, then halfway following the liquid shape

which water makes through land,
always the distances expanding,

a home so faraway it can't be seized,
intangible as winter through the trees.

THIRD GENERATION

We dream of falling as we fall
                  asleep, but wake to feel
the weight of quilts, our pillows chill

        as granite to the cheek.
What science calls the hypnic jerk—
                 a heartbeat slows too quickly

in the body's cage, air ripped,
          lynched half between the lips
and ribs. We know that memory skips

               some families like a stone
across a lake. They sleep alone.
        But we, the chosen ones,

are chosen for a crowded sleep,
                each night compelled to leap
the barbed wire ledge, a heap

          of limbs. We somersault
to spill ourselves on basalt
        slabs below. It's not our fault,

this twitch of muscles snapping us
        from rest, electric pulse
so like descent we drop weightless

until we flinch awake,
so sure of death that we mistake
our nightmares for the ache

of breaking bone.

MY MOTHER, MAKING PIROSHKE

There was an instinct in her touch I tried
to imitate—I let one hand follow
the other into the flesh of the dough,
like a baby kneading in its mother's side
before it curves close to a dream of milk.
She rolled the dough more flexible than cloth,
as if it weren't our dinner but something soft
to hug against the skin, a piece of silk
that's slept beneath. Then she held a water glass,
pressing its mouth into the countertop,
pale flourings of O's. She always stopped
to cradle each within her palm, a last
moment (open, unfilled) before she spooned
the meat inside and sealed the crescent moon.

BAGGAGE

For years my fingers stumbled on
the lock, as if I hadn't seen
a thousand times my mother's hands
turning the fetus-key, a bone

of gold she must have excised from
my wrist. I watched her lift the lid.
She smoothed a dress already smooth
from never being worn. We held

our family snapshots to the lamp,
each face a smoke and skull x-ray
against the glare. Sometimes she showed
me coins sewn into hems, displayed

five currencies for five escapes
we hadn't made but might, the right
disaster waiting to be born.
Even America could not

fix DNA, defect that made
us find the door in any space,
a gene that warned me when to slide
the suitcase from its hiding place,

papers and Shabbes candlesticks
already packed, an exit route
conceived before my birth, before
adrenaline: my instinct out.

A BRIEF ONTOLOGY OF GUILT

No pill could numb the ache
      that kept my grandmother awake
each night, the gray fingers
           of insomnia lingering
like a dybbuk's hand against her cheek.
         I remember weeks
my mother paced the hall,
             her footfalls
hammering the ashwood floor,
      the sound of slammed and opened drawers
while she looked…for what?
      A box of bleached letters, a silver locket
clasping pictures of the dead,
         their faces smudged, their heads
tiny as stars seen through a telescope.
            What did she hope
to find? And I—tattooed inside
      my dreams, choking on cyanide—
what use were my night terrors?
         In that house speech was rarer
even than relief from pain. We paled with shock,
      joints like cracked limestone, knees locked
at acute angles, toes turned
         to marble claws. *Trauma*, a wound burned
in the body
      or written there as though we three
were parchment. Even morning's yellow
        glow
sickened into jaundice, white
           paint reflecting light,

almost medicinal though not
                    a cure for silence, our eyes bloodshot
with grains of sleep, our skin
          translucent as a lampshade, paper-thin.

ALWAYS ALREADY

Survivors never tell their progeny—
    We are always already
               winter
       in the hinterlands,
    always already the Pale
of Settlement, always the wailing
widow at her husband's grave
      or else there is no grave,
no headstone where he died, and we are searching
             through the birches
      for a sign.
    We are always resigned
to be the mountain made of shoes,
    always the everlasting bruise
of magic numbers, always
the prophets of our own blazing,
    our self-consuming star. We are
        and always were the puckered scar
    that never disappears
beneath the skin. Or does it reappear
each time we think it almost gone,
    rising to the surface like a stone
that will not sink for all its heaviness?
We are always already dressed
      for our own funeral march.
         Look how our bodies lurch
as though still traveling on the train.
    We are always already trained
      to speak and never speak

of it, to never speak obliquely
as a curving track,
and never turn our bodies to look back.

LOT'S WIFE IN EASTERN EUROPE

Why salt? I say she turned
   to be preservative,
      to keep her past from rotting,
her slender daughters brazed

as rods of soldered iron.
   She watched the primitive
      shul collapse—first walls caught
fire, and then doorways,

at last the roof. She yearned
   for castoff things: a sieve,
      a spoon, a favorite teapot,
a porcelain platter glazed

like melted glass. *Return*
   was an imperative
      and salt the afterthought
of tears. She stood in haze,

her body almost burning.
   This is what ruin gives
      its witnesses—eyes hot
from standing near the blaze.

KOSHER DILLS

In the Scroll of Ruth, Naomi
kvetches her way to Bethlehem,

each tear like vinegar, each step
seeding the dirt with sorrow plants.

I went out full, she weeps to Ruth.
And even though she eats a sack

of dates along the way, her gut
spills over pickle-sourness.

Naomi can't forget her years
as refugee, how bitterness

brined her name while others called
her sweet, her mothertongue preserved

to keep its tart and liquid flesh.
Perhaps she grieves in the Yiddish

of my family, a bottled song,
the garlic words of those who fled

but thirsted for return, asking
for fruit but tasting salt instead.

PTEROMERHANOPHOBIA

Washington Dulles Airport

No wonder that we falter at the gate
       or that the graveled words have settled in our throats.

We cross, fumble for boarding pass, passport,
       not leaving for the underworld but that

above, a vapor-world where breath gasps out
       through yellow masks and seat cushions float.

For safety we remove our shoes, unknot
       laces slowly as though our skin should not

go bare. We cross the line that separates
       our rooted selves from wings. Of course, we shut

our eyes against a wind which only beats
       in memory. Of course, we can't forget

what we have heard of flying through the night:
       how darkness feathers in the dark, how feet

stumble but never feel the weight of dirt,
       how we depart from what we love but cannot part.

3

GOING SOUTH

Our route drives parallel to the north/south train.
My guide explains the storks we see, perching

on platforms linked by power lines, are free to nest
on any property in Poland, protected for the luck

they bring to families—the crossing of red beaks
at mating time, a sign of strawberries in June,

and tracks of fallen feathers by the road, a rune
predicting money from the sky. They fly to Africa

in the fall, follow the heated thread of thermals
across the thin neck of the Bosphorus,

returning early spring before the Lenten fast.
They used to roost in Wolski forest, white bodies

hidden by black rows of oak. But once they flew
those woods, drifting like chimney smoke along

the slate rooftops, they didn't stop to feed again.
Some Poles believe that soon the storks will leave

for good, sent south along the railroad tracks,
beyond the vanishing point, and won't come back.

WITH THE INTERPRETER

He talks for me as we drive south. Or tries.
At a roadside stand, where we have stopped to buy

the latest crop of blackberries, I see
he winces at a stranger's inquiry,

tells me the woman asks about my hair,
if I was born with curls, a style so rare

down here, she guesses that I had to twist
the strands into metallic springs. I miss

the knife-edge of my voice, how it once sliced
such questions straight to bone and blood, no nice

distinctions made. My answer would have mashed
her tongue, the Polish word for what she asks,

so close to *yid*, it's clear she wants to know
if I should be deciphered as a Jew.

      We dark-starred foreigners,

it's not our speech that needs a translator—
the woman understands my coins, gestures

for me to pick a crate of fruit, replies
you're welcome when I thank her with my eyes.

It's not our speech but that our mouths are shaped
to lacerate the silences. We're scraped

from the soil of other countrysides,
those flinted hills, a language that divides.

THE IZAAK SYNAGOGUE

In Kazimierz, the old Jewish section
of Kraków, Poland

We found the Synagogue on Honey Street
but sweetness didn't sit beneath our tongues,
not when the only Jew who davened there
was black and white: a life-sized cardboard man,
a Hasid from another century
who bent black-coated toward the missing Ark,
bowing, as if half-risen from his seat
and waiting for a prayer to be sung.
Hard to forget his face. But tourists stared
at him then hurried to their caravans,
rushing perhaps to the next oddity.
A kosher meal? A klezmer band? The dark
locations where the ghetto used to rot?
Hard to forget this place. And yet it's not.

SOUVENIR

In Kraków's marketplace, the kiosks vend
carved men at thirty złotys each: a Jew
who grips the Torah in his wooden hands,
a beggar Jew, a bobble-headed Jew
whose body sways and nods with just a pull
against his jagged nose, a singing Jew,
a Jew who spills gold coins onto a scale,
the balance tipping in his favor. These Jews
will be wrapped up and taken home to stand
on cluttered shelves. Children will clench the Jews,
the *żydki*, as their parents say. How pale
their faces are, how dark the beards of Jews,
as black as coal dust covering new snow
(and lost with memory in the dirt below).

REHMUH SYNAGOGUE, POLAND

I prayed beside survivors too:
those wives who sighed the liturgy
behind a lacy screen, turning
the pages of their siddurim

too quietly to call it noise,
a shadow-touch of fingertips
as might have pushed an uncurled strand
of hair beneath its wig again.

What did they ask of *Adonai*
that Friday night?—more light perhaps,
two candles lit by smoother hands,
each match strike startling back the dark.

A room away, their husbands stood
so quickly wooden benches creaked
like bones. Inside the women's section,
no one could watch red curtains pulled

to show the Arc, could only feel
all breaths-becoming-one, exhaled
in speech as *Hear, O Israel*.
The Torah never reached that space

where wives stayed still enough to hear
beyond the wall dividing them,
the laughter of their men whose arms
stretched out to greet the *Shabbes* bride.

ICON OF THE BLACK MADONNA

Częstochowa, Poland

Poor thing—she took an arrow to the throat,
then robbers stripped the stones that lined her frame.
They slashed her twice across the cheek. Restored,

she showed these cuts despite ten coats of paint
and never healed, preferring to recall
each sacrilegious touch. Like other girls,

she learned that scars could make her beautiful.
One time she chose to save the town, chasing
three thousand Swedes away. Her eyes could break

a man or heal him of his sins. Sometimes
she watched while armies rumbled through.
As for her face, it's black from candle smoke

and age, or black because she's Byzantine,
or black because she's seen the darkness crawl
like spiders on her skin, and can't forget.

OLD TOWN

In Warsaw: reconstructed
from rubble in the decade after WWII

Real history could never look so good.
Instead, patinas have been painted on
to show false wear on walls that haven't stood
five centuries of dust and human touch,
just fifty years of tourist industry.
If *prawda* signifies the truth, not much
is true when every ancient coat of arms,
each red-tiled roof, each Art Nouveau *salon*
de thé was turned out in a factory,
trompe l'œil to double-cross the eye or charm
vacationers. The locals know a con:
the new-made-old, 3-D enough to last.
But even they prefer a forgery
to walking through the ruins of the past.

AT THE HOLOCAUST CONFERENCE

Strawberry jam helps choke our breakfast down.
Between the picked-clean bones of Paul Celan
and vultures by the coffee pot (well so-and-so
can't sink his teeth in tenure even though
he's eaten crow) it seems atrocity
demands the appetite of PhDs,
an all-devouring works-cited page
to explicate our taste for ash. What rage
for scholarship. Blood-lettered nametags call,
Hello, My Name Is Expert In The Fall
Of Auschwitz-Birkenau. By dinnertime,
the Zyklon B will mix with sips of wine,
a Riesling with a vineyard-peach bouquet.
No business like the Shoah Biz, we say.

CHARM AGAINST A BROKEN TONGUE

When words erased the need
for ink, blank pages fluttered like a winding sheet

and *mama-loshn* crumbled into dust.
That is, the *mother tongue* smelled of must:

unopened prayer shawls pinned flat
against the wall like butterflies. *Aleph* and *bet*

took wing as raven-messengers, letters
with claws too blunt to disinter

the world. To touch the dead is *treyf*. To touch dead verse,
what then? What of the Edelshteins cursing

with faded words, a poetry
which cannot stand the light? This Hall of Oddities—

the *yad* points toward a book that isn't there,
a silver finger gesturing at air.

ALL SAINTS' DAY

After Czesław Miłosz

Someone is always kneeling at a grave
or burning votives at the gate.
Small cups of light begin November's days.

Then in the church, our voices answer *Pray
for us*, because some ends are fated,
more certain than chrysanthemums that fade

in autumn, growing brittle in the cold.
When mourners weep about old wounds,
their words like poppy seeds across the ground,

the ghosts will masquerade as butcherbirds.
As for the dead, they do not hurt.
They cannot feel the crushing weight of dirt.

When death goes through our house, we open all
the doors, turn mirrors toward the wall
to ward off souls. *Leave us. Leave us alone.*

THE STONE I FOUND AT AUSCHWITZ

doesn't want to be in poetry.
The stone isn't orange as amber
picked from the Baltic. It doesn't glow
beer-bottle-green like sea glass. Or gleam
bright red like a bright red, coral bead.
But squats, ash-gray, bending like a bean
that's been squeezed between finger and thumb.

I found it on the gravel walk, near
the Wall of Death—one of the many
squat and graying, the ignored stones I saw.
I couldn't take them all. This one fit
as if cut to the map of my palm.
In my hand, I held what was no more
than stone and left through the front gates.

YAHRZEIT

In Galicia, now southern Poland

In the land of goyim,
I burn a candle for you,
my only light, a pot
of saints—red crackle glass,
a prayer embossed
on the jar. I sing a hymn.
The cotton wick glows blue,
white paraffin so hot
it puddles clear.
                    It's not
the vessel of the flame
that counts, but how sorrow
strikes its match in us. Loss
is loss: a sudden spark,
and just as suddenly, the dark.

4

FASTING

The tongue will recreate the taste of juice,
sipping on prayers made hot with black pepper
and swallowing a rough-edged word like *sin*—
it asks for utterance but scrapes the throat.
The world-to-come is body without pain.
But here, the body learns itself through tests:
a palm burned by a pot, an eye turned toward
the sun, a woman pressed against a man.
Heat and friction teach what food cannot,
except the food of speech, fat sentences
that sate the mouth by spilling out.
There is a space between some legs. The gut
needs emptiness in order to be filled.
A hand holds tight before it learns release.

THE AMBER BROOCH

It's true that there are tears in things—
   for instance, the brooch I bring

back from Kraków, which pricks
   my fingertip the first time that I fix

it to my shirt.
   And later, when I touch the clasp, my finger hurts

again. Some pains return.
   Some tears turn

sepia with age, stubborn as the Baltic
   or the resin dragonfly, an insect

that summons flight
   in the very shape of its body. It lights

on my collar as if to wait
   for breezes near the shore and hesitates,

the way I do, each time my hand remembers reaching
   past garnets red as bee stings

to sort through amber at the vendor's booth.
   In Poland, I held the proof

that there's an elegy in every hammered hinge and catch,
   the lacy filigree, the closure that latches

like an entrance
   to a tiny room, beauty and balance

sharpened to a point, the silver pin,
  which leaves a spot of blood where it has been.

MEZUZAH

Look closely at the metal sleeve, a case
no bigger than my thumb. You'll see it shows
a month of prints: some dirt I carried in

under my nails or dust I carried out,
a trace of flour from bread I baked,
and inky spots from messages I wrote.

Write them upon the doorposts of thy house
and on thy gates. In Deuteronomy,
we Jews are told that even entrances

and exits from the home must have their rules.
If only habit could convert to faith.
My fingertips have brushed the case, a touch

as quick, unthinking as a gust of wind
across the water's surface. I've kissed my hand,
returned the blessing to my lips, hoping

a taste would help me understand our laws.
The rabbis say that guards cannot protect
a king, but Torah keeps a beggar safe.

Beneath the silver lid, a parchment scroll
is rolled too tight to let in disbelief,
the prayer facing in upon itself,

the words like lovers in a darkened room.
A name of God is written on the square—
I cannot see it, but I know it's there.

ROSH HASHANAH

By following my voice back to its source,
I found the shofar's open mouth, a call
to men inside the belly of a fish,
to barren wives and husbands building boats,
to wrestlers, to weeping ones who've lost
the liquid crunch of seeds, a wisdom fruit
between their teeth, and later lost the world,
to those who asked the whirlwind *Why?* I found
a calendar that celebrates new songs—
the same songs every year but funneling
through me (a channeled throat), made new again.
I found the apple-heart. The days were marked
in red and found by listening for the blasts.
I filled my lungs to fill the air with words.

OSSUARY

to her little brother

I.
It is like a woman to love boxes
         for the spaces kept inside: a room to hold
what's left behind
                  and maybe that's enough

of explanation but maybe not for you.
         When I'm dead, if words can weight the hand,
please carry me across the cobblestones,

past crowds into St. Mary's Church to stand
         before the altarpiece of agonies,
carved martyrs kept alive in gold. A fog

will catch your throat
                  you never crossed yourself
         with *Father, Son,* or *Holy Ghost,* to see
if it felt good. Then cup the brass
                  the box

while Kaddish turns your mouth to ash and dust
         to dust
                  because I questioned whirlwinds once.

2.
In 1988, I ate beet soup

one block away. The broth steamed burgundy,
            so pepper-sharp it stung my tongue. I drank
a glass of tea
                    played make believe my eyes

were blue not brown, sucked sugar cubes
            which melted like the Host between my teeth.
You were two when Daddy brought me here by train,

came down to see DaVinci's Ermine Lady
            but she was ransomed in the War.
We walked, not going where we should have gone

the synagogues, the town known as Oświęcim.

3.
            Now take the spiral staircase, winding up
then back upon itself to spire's top

to sky to balcony to trumpeter.
            Before your birth I read the fairy tale
of music played to warn of an attack:

"The Tatar's arrow knew the straightest lines.
            An archer waxed the thread. His thumb could pull
the bowstring back and pull it back again.

How fast the flight—shaft quavering,
            smoothing as target neared, a voice that found
its pitch against the windpipe of a trumpeter."

Eight hundred years ago an arrowed death
            came mid-refrain
                            or was it yesterday?

4.
In my first months at university, I tried

to be a better Jew. To be a Jew
            I stood in Temple Sinai and heard
the shofar blow its hundred blasts
                            hoping

I'd recognize a hundred echoings
            within my caverned heart. When Oma died
in Florida
            you were too young to watch

I saw her coffin lowered in the hole.
            She couldn't hear the mud rise in my throat
from Hebrew words I didn't understand,

Yit-ga-dal ve-yit-ka-dash she-mei ra-ba,
            Glorified and sanctified be God's great name.
I left a pebble on her grave, left

behind this death
                    hating the granite stone
            that held her down. Then once again in Poland,
I walked the camps where relatives were killed,

the breezes barely breathing through the grass,
            as old and accented as Oma's voice

in her stories of the War
                              the poisoned fish

that sent her father to the hospital
                    where doctors wouldn't touch a dirty Jew,
her father's deathbed messages to *Go*. That night,

I dreamed my body burned
                                             not quite nightmare
                    as it might sound. I remembered Oma's grave,
only to know I'd make my grave in air.

5.
Now to remember or to give the dead
                    a second life, a man replays the tune.
At noon, a pause between weather and news.

He lifts the horn. Music sounds best beside him,
                    Old Town a tattered aquatint that's wet with ink,
the pink streaked black, the blur of avenues.

                    In far-off Warsaw on the radio,
you'd hear the broken note
                                             but never know
                    the trumpeter sees Tatars at the gates.

                    He plays and plays, until he wakes the world
and wakes the arrow that closed his throat.

6.
            If words have any weight, perhaps you'll ask

What is the uncut line between the train
            she took, the bowl of soup, the sugar cubes,
the klezmer violins she didn't hear,

            the tour of Auschwitz that she didn't take
for years, the portrait of a lady?
                              I held
            you on your second day, your head became

the making of my hand, its river-curves.
            One day you'll wonder if I left the Jew
beneath a cobblestone. Conflicted in

itself, Kraków shows lives on top of lives.

7.
            In the rest after melody, the dead
will almost live. The town, crammed as a mind

with memory, empties itself of shame.
            What other explanation can I give?
The view is beautiful, the streets drawn fine

            as the lines in your palm. Remove the lid.
Tip the urn into the current. Handfuls
            of ash will catch the wind to paint the flow

in dizzy wheels, spinning like a fugue above
          the flower stalls, rising toward the hill
to circle and rise higher, as high as

          the university, the outer walls
and railway, running past the railway
          like the ghost of cattle cars, weaving through

barbed wire, across the bone fields, to weave
          beneath the fences and spill out, freed to
the riverbanks and mixing with the sea.

BASIA
Warsaw, 2002

Twelve years ago, I was the little girl
who watched her work. She cleaned my parents' house,
cooked meals, took care of me. I learned from her
a soft language, each phrase sounding like *hush*

and the swishing shut of my bedroom door.
Now when we meet, phrases I used to speak,
easily as swallowing mint tea, taste strange.
Words are stale on my tongue and stick.

We stand beneath a farmer's tree to steal
his pears. Taller, I reach the higher boughs.
Small, smaller than I thought, she shakes the trunk
then laughs as sweet, green fruits tumble down.

She shook me once like this. When I was five,
a butterscotch stuck sideways in my throat.
Her arms felt strong from lifting pots of soup
and kneading dough or maybe I felt light,

the breath kept from my lungs. I was her sack
after the shops. Upended. Emptied out.
We must have both breathed then. Against the floor,
an amber candy glistened with my spit.

SUKKOT

Folded in half, crumpled, or quickly cut,
our will is tethered to the sand, a tent
on shifting ground. We listen for the storms,
the unseen finger-winds that rearrange
the dunes and nudge the stars into new shapes.
No map. We walk for forty years, always
half-lost but following the clouds by day
or flames that write directions on the night.
The Archer's arrow arches through the sky
until it spears the Scorpion. We find
what certainty there is—the constancy
of yellow hills that move like bodies twined
in bed, confused but slow to shake this sleep,
asleep but waking to another dream.

JUDAIC STUDIES

University of Nebraska-Lincoln

The department doesn't even fill a floor
but one room at the university,
fluorescents dark behind a frosted door
which answers woodenly to every knock.
No secretary waiting there to call
me *puppele*, German for little doll,
or feed me raspberry-swirled rugelach,
the sweetness now an eaten memory.
On certain days, Nebraska could be Poland,
the same blond silences of plains, each field
a golden corridor that never ends.
What happened to the open door? It's sealed,
with every light turned off, and no one home
except the wind breathing *alone, alone.*

AT MEL KRUPIN'S

Jewish deli, Washington, D.C.

It's always a feast day here, forever
the appetite
which comes after a fast: chopped liver,
the calm simplicity of black-and-white
cookies, whose icing gleams
with shadow and its opposite, no in-between, plastic
bowls of kosher dills, perspiring cans of cream
soda or celery tonic
to sing and fizzle down the throat,
always corn beef, thin-cut
as pages from a prayer book, translucent whisper on the rye,
cheese blintzes pale beneath their coats
of cherry sauce, always donuts,
and luminous wedges of keylime pie.

TASHLIKH

a casting away of sins at Rosh Hashanah

What if the New Year brings a second choice?
—no more amnesia when the shofar's voice
calls out to us, but memory stacked thick
and dog-eared in our hands as prayer books.
This time, we'll scribble sins on grocery lists,
on notes passed back and forth in class, pissed-off
petitions to the president, or reams
of poetry upon a favorite theme.
And we will only speak in present tense.
We'll tear weak words from lexicons, dispense
with *shame* and *bystander.* Our tongues will bleed.
We'll scatter breadcrumbs at the sea to feed
the fish. We'll fling our yesterdays
into the night and watch their starlit blaze.

DISCUSSING MIŁOSZ

A red wing rose in the darkness.
—"Encounter"

After the red bird rises through the night,
it leaves a wing-shaped shadow on the sky.

The teacher asks, *If the field is dark
how can the poet see red flight?* and would like

one of the boys (his baseball cap pulled low
over his eyes) to answer that we know

the color of our blood from memory.
We don't need light. A girl would reply

the bird predicts both darting hare and man
whose gesture follows, a lightning run

of fur and tail, the sleek hind legs to leap
into the third couplet where we skip

across the years, both hare and man now gone,
only their motions left behind. And then

like sudden grassfire the class would understand
the poet's awe, why he writes these words instead

of weeping, why the poem must streak by,
bleeding and animal but not quick to die.

Notes

The Language Thief
Eating bitter herbs, drinking salt water, and saying the words "next year in Jerusalem," are all ritual elements of the Passover seder, a meal which commemorates the exodus of the Israelites from Egypt.

The Izaak Synagogue
Daven comes from Yiddish, meaning "to pray." Klezmer is secular, Jewish folk music.

Rehmuh Synagogue, Poland
In Orthodox synagogues, women sit in a separate section, often curtained or screened off from the rest of the sanctuary. Siddurim is the plural of siddur, a Jewish prayer book. Adonai is one of the Hebrew names for god. "Hear, O Israel" is a translation of the first line of a Hebrew prayer known as the Sh'ma, the most important prayer in Judaism.

Charm Against a Broken Tongue
Mama-loshn, meaning mother-tongue, is the Yiddish word for the language of Yiddish. Aleph and bet are the first two letters of the Hebrew alphabet, from which come the word "alphabet." Treyf is the Hebrew term for unkosher, that is, for foods not prepared according to Jewish law. Edelshtein is the protagonist of Cynthia Ozick's short story, "Envy; or Yiddish In America," which depicts the failure of an immigrant Yiddish poet to find a translator and rescue his work from obscurity.

Yahrzeit
Yahrzeit means "time of a year" in Yiddish. A yahrzeit candle is burned on the anniversary of a loved one's death.

Fasting
Fasting plays an significant part in many Jewish holy days but is particularly important during Yom Kippur, the Day of Atonement.

Rosh Hashanah
Rosh Hashanah is the Jewish New Year. The shofar is a trumpet made from a ram's horn, which is blown during Rosh Hashanah.

Ossuary
Section Four: "Yit-ga-dal ve-yit-ka-dash she-mei ra-ba" is a transliteration of the opening of the mourner's Kaddish, an Aramaic blessing that figures prominently in Jewish funerals, prayer services, and memorials.

Sukkot
Sukkot is a Jewish harvest festival; for this holiday, Jews construct temporary structures to commemorate the huts in which the Israelites lived during their 40 years of wandering after the exodus from Egypt.

Judaic Studies
Rugelach is a Jewish pastry, generally containing raisins, chocolate, or some other kind of sweet filling.

Tashlikh
Tashlikh is a traditional practice on Rosh Hashanah. In a symbolic discarding of the previous year's sins, participants toss pieces of paper or chunks of bread into a natural body of moving water, such as a stream or river.

About the Poet

Jehanne Dubrow was born in Italy and grew up in Poland, Yugoslavia, Zaire, Belgium, Austria, and the United States. She earned her PhD in English and creative writing from the University of Nebraska-Lincoln and her MFA in poetry from the University of Maryland, College Park. She served as a Sosland Foundation Fellow at the Center for Advanced Holocaust Studies and has received scholarships from the Sewanee Writers' Conference, the West Chester Poetry Conference, the Nebraska Summer Writers' Conference, the Auschwitz Jewish Center, and the Institute on the Holocaust and Jewish Civilization.

Additional Three Candles Press Titles

Matthew Shindell: *In Another Castle*
Release Date: Nov. 11, 2008
104 Pages, $13.95, ISBN: 978-0-9770892-5-3

Erin Elizabeth Smith: *The Fear of Being Found*
Release Date: Feb. 15, 2008
85 Pages, $13.95, ISBN: 978-0-9770892-4-6

Andrew Demcak: *Catching Tigers in Red Weather*
Release Date: Oct. 30, 2007
88 Pages, $13.95, ISBN: 978-0-9770892-3-9

Tony Trigilio: *The Lama's English Lessons*
Release Date: Nov. 30, 2006
96 Pages, $12.95, ISBN: 0-9770892-1-5

RJ McCaffery: *Ice Sculpture of Mermaid With Cigar*
Release Date: April 7, 2006
128 Pages, $12.95, ISBN: 0-9770892-0-7

Digerati: 20 Contemporary Poets in the Virtual World
Release Date: February 21, 2006
336 pages, price $15.95, ISBN: 0-9770892-2-3

Titles are available through Ingram and Small Press Distribution.

Printed in the United States
137250LV00004B/22/P